BLESSED NAMES

WHY WAS HE NAMED AL-JAWAD (A)?

WRITTEN BY:

KISA KIDS PUBLICATIONS

Please recite a Fātiḥah for the marḥūmīn
of the Rangwala family, the sponsors of this book.

All proceeds from the sale of this book
will be used to produce more educational resources.

Dedication

This book is dedicated to the beloved Imām of our time (AJ). May Allāh (swt) hasten his reappearance and help us become his true companions.

Acknowledgements

Prophet Muḥammad (s): The pen of a writer is mightier than the blood of a martyr.

True reward lies with Allāh, but we would like to sincerely thank Shaykh Salim Yusufali and Sisters Sabika Mithar Liliana Villalvazo, Zahra Sabur, Kisae Nazar, Sarah Assaf, Nadia Dossani, Fatima Hussain, Naseem Rangwala, ar Zehra Abbas. We would especially like to thank Nainava Publications for their contributions. May Allāh bless them this world and the next.

Preface

Prophet Muḥammad (s): Nurture and raise your children in the best way. Raise them with the love of the Prophe and the Ahl al-Bayt (a).

Literature is an influential form of media that often shapes the thoughts and views of an entire generation. Therefor in order to establish an Islamic foundation for the future generations, there is a dire need for compelling Islam literature. Over the past several years, this need has become increasingly prevalent throughout Islamic centers ar schools everywhere. Due to the growing dissonance between parents, children, society, and the teachings of Islā and the Ahl al-Bayt (a), this need has become even more pressing. Al-Kisa Foundation, along with its subsidiary, Kis Kids Publications, was conceived in an effort to help bridge this gap with the guidance of ʿulamah and the help educators. We would like to make this a communal effort and platform. Therefore, we sincerely welcome constructiv feedback and help in any capacity.

The goal of the *Blessed Names* series is to help children form a lasting bond with the 14 Māʿṣūmīn by learnir about and connecting with their names. We hope that you and your children enjoy these books and use them as means to achieve this goal, inshā'Allāh. We pray to Allāh to give us the strength and tawfīq to perform our duties ar responsibilities.

With Duʾās,
Nabi R. Mir (Abidi)

Kisa Kids Publications
4415 Fortran Court
San Jose, CA 95134
(260) KISA-KID [547-2543]

An Introduction to the Blessed Names

Our names are a very special part of us. Many times, they shape our personalities and even explain who we are or the person we would like to become. In this series, you will explore the names and titles of our beloved 14 Ma'soomeen. Did you know that their names and titles were not just ordinary names? They were special because they were given to them by Allah!

Allah has given seven special heavenly names to our Ma'soomeen: Muhammad, Ali, Fatimah, Hasan, Husain, Ja'far, and Musa. Behind each of these names is a heavenly power!

In addition to their names, each of the Ma'soomeen also had special titles by which they became famous. Their titles were often given to them because of the circumstances of their time, but these titles and characteristics were common amongst all the Ma'soomeen. For example, Imam al-Baqir (a) was known for spreading knowledge because he was able to create many new universities and branches of knowledge during his time. However, if the other Ma'soomeen had the same opportunity, they, too, would have spread knowledge and created universities in their teaching circles. In these stories, you will discover some of the reasons why the Ma'soomeen received their specific names or titles.

Many of us share our names with these beloved Ma'soomeen or know people who do. Let's learn about these blessed names and titles so we can strive to be like our blessed Ma'soomeen!

I think al-Jawad means...

_____

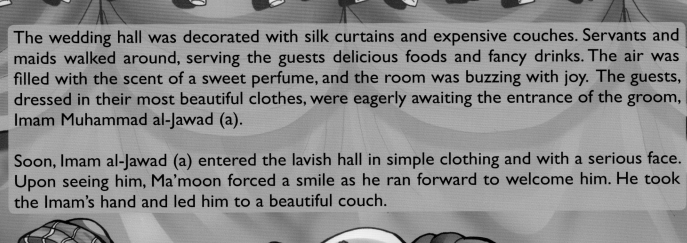

The wedding hall was decorated with silk curtains and expensive couches. Servants and maids walked around, serving the guests delicious foods and fancy drinks. The air was filled with the scent of a sweet perfume, and the room was buzzing with joy. The guests, dressed in their most beautiful clothes, were eagerly awaiting the entrance of the groom, Imam Muhammad al-Jawad (a).

Soon, Imam al-Jawad (a) entered the lavish hall in simple clothing and with a serious face. Upon seeing him, Ma'moon forced a smile as he ran forward to welcome him. He took the Imam's hand and led him to a beautiful couch.

On the other side of the beautiful golden curtain, the women sat around Ma'moon's daughter, Um al-Fadhl, who would soon become Imam al-Jawad's wife. While this may have *looked* like the perfect wedding, it was all just a clever trick by the evil caliph, Ma'moon. You see, Ma'moon forced Imam al-Jawad (a) to marry his daughter so he could keep the Imam (a) close to him and make sure that he didn't overthrow Ma'moon's kingdom.

As the wedding ceremony began, the Imam (a) sadly read his own aqd of nikaah. When the nikaah was finished, everyone began clapping loudly and happily, except the Imam (a). You see, Imam al-Jawad (a) knew that this wedding was all just part of Ma'moon's evil plans. However, no one else seemed to notice the sad look on the Imam's face.

Ma'moon wanted everyone to think he was very generous, so he ordered the servants to bring out large plates filled with rice, meat, fruits, and desserts of all kinds. Once all the guests had eaten more than they could handle, Ma'moon signaled for his servants to bring out the surprise gifts.

The servants, dressed in special uniforms, came from all corners of the room, holding trays filled with small golden boxes. They handed them to the excited guests, who couldn't wait to tear open the boxes and see what was inside!

Inside each box, there was a special note on which the caliph had written an "I owe you" note. These notes stated that the guests would receive either gold bars, silver coins, or even a house! The guests couldn't believe their eyes and were overcome with excitement! However, everyone soon began wondering what was written on each other's papers, and some started to feel envious of others.

But before they could say anything, another set of servants came out, passing out bags of gold coins to each guest. Everyone became even happier and started praising and thanking Ma'moon, not knowing that he was doing all of this just to show off.

For a third time, another set of servants came out. This time, they were carrying plates shaped like boats with very expensive perfumes. Each guest sprayed themselves with the beautiful scents.

Just then, Ma'moon called for everyone's attention. The guests fell silent, excited for Ma'moon's big announcement! Ma'moon reached for a long scroll of paper and began reading out loud all the items he would be gifting Imam al-Jawad (a). You would think that the Imam (a) would be thrilled with all the gifts he was getting, but Imam al-Jawad (a) did not seem happy at all! He knew that Ma'moon's intentions were not sincere. However, the guests were in awe over all the gifts he was to receive. After Ma'moon finished speaking, the guests clapped joyfully, astonished at how generous Ma'moon had been.

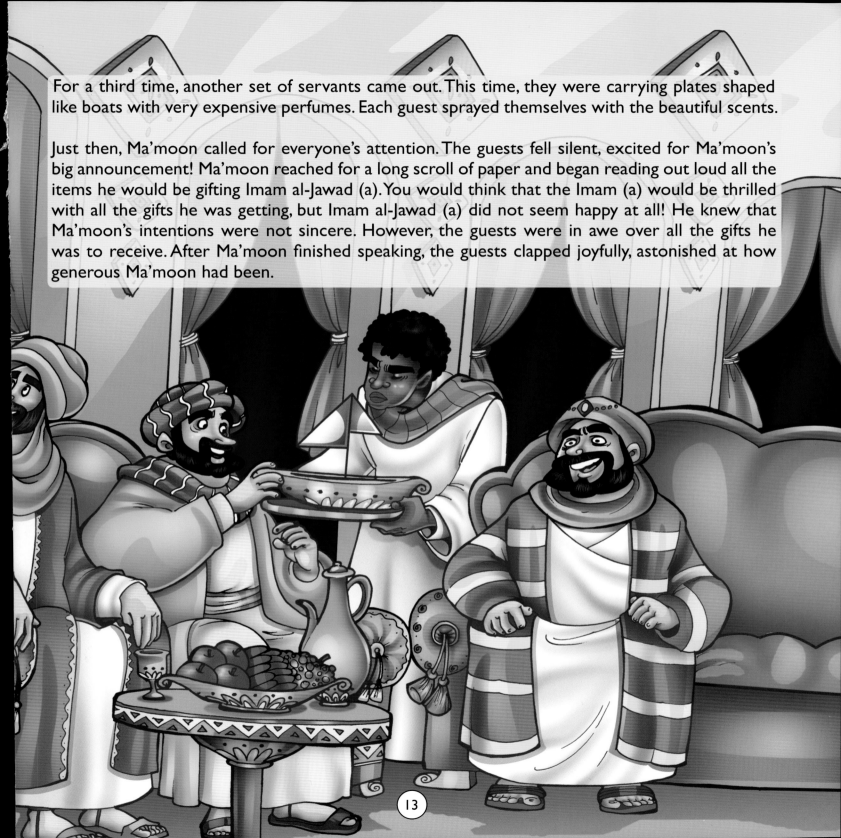

As the wedding came to an end, the guests clutched their gifts close to their chests and left the party feeling overjoyed with everything they had received.

How foolish the guests had been! You see, Ma'moon's generosity was fake. He had stolen most of his money and thought that by giving it away, the people would think he was a generous and kind caliph. He did not understand that real generosity is when someone gives out of their own belongings to the needy only for the sake of Allah.

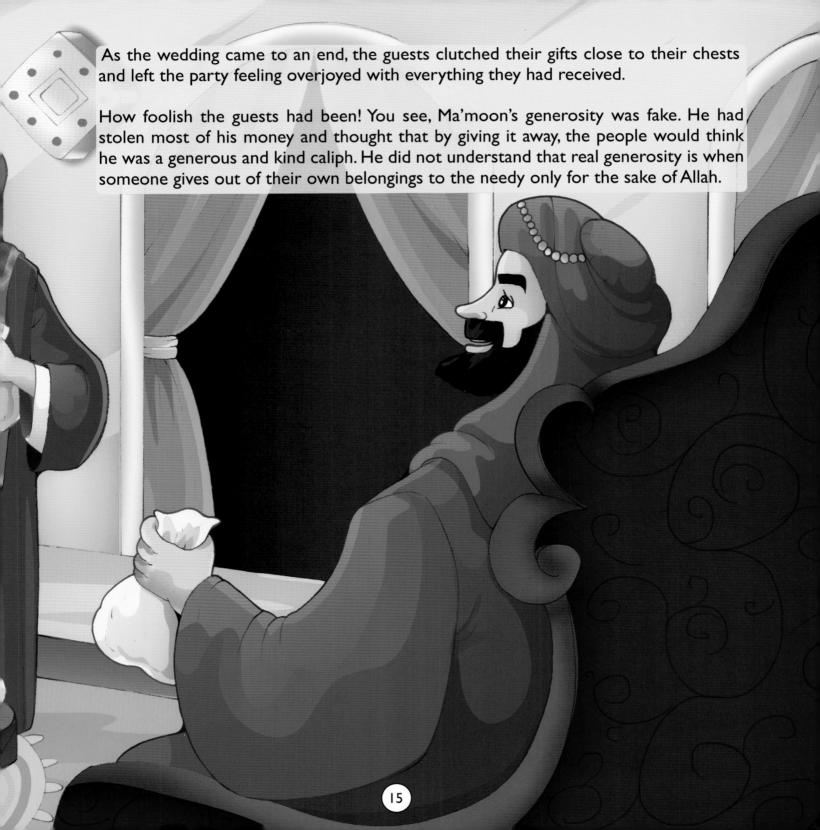

You see, it was really Imam al-Jawad (a) who showed us what true generosity is. When the Imam (a) went to Mecca, he took all of his wealth and divided it amongst the poor and needy. After Hajj, he decided to leave Khorasaan and return to his hometown, Medina. He left the lavish castle that Ma'moon had given him, and instead found a small, simple home to live in. He was happier in this small home, where he spent all his time praying and showing kindness to others.

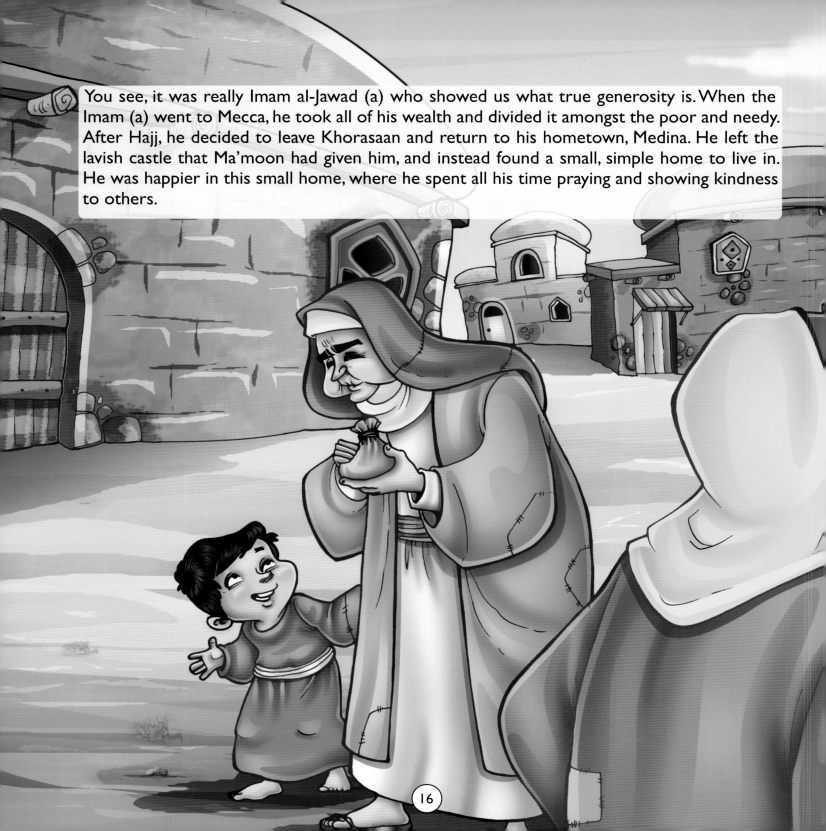

One day, some of Imam al-Jawad's companions from Khorasaan came to visit him. When they entered the Imam's simple house, they were shocked! The Imam's home in Khorasaan had been so much more grand and magnificent! It had everything you could imagine, but this house only had one simple carpet on the floor!